GRANTED

GRANTED

MARY
SZYBIST

ALICE JAMES BOOKS

Farmington, Maine

Alice James Books are published by Alice James Poetry Cooperative, Inc.,
an affiliate of the University of Maine at Farmington.

Alice James Books
114 Prescott Street
Farmington, ME 04938

www.alicejamesbooks.org

Epigraph text from *The Brothers Karamazov* by Fyodor Dostoyevsky, edited
by Manuel Komroff, translated by Constance Garnett, copyright © 1957 by
Manuel Komroff. Used by permission of Dutton Signet, a division of Pen-
guin Putnam, Inc.

Epigraph text from *Women in their Beds* by Gina Berriault © 1996 by Gina
Berriault. Reprinted by permission of Counterpoint Press, a member of
Perseus Books, L.L.C.

Epigraph text from *Gravity and Grace* by Simone Weil, translated by
Arthur Wills, copyright 1952, renewal © 1980 by G.P. Putnam's Sons.
Original French copyright 1947 by Librairie Plon. Used by permission of
G.P. Putnam's Sons, a division of Penguin Putnam, Inc.

Library of Congress Cataloging-in-Publication Data

Szybist, Mary, 1970-
Granted / Mary Szybist.
p. cm.
ISBN 1-882295-37-4
I. Title.
PS3619.Z93 G73 2003
811'.6--dc21

2002015865

Alice James Book gratefully acknowledges support from the University of Maine
at Farmington and the National Endowment for the Arts.

Cover Art: Burne-Jones, Edward (1833–1896). The Mirror of Venus. 1898 (detail).
Museu Calouste Gulbenkian, Lisbon, Portugal
Copyright Art Resource, NY

ACKNOWLEDGMENTS

Grateful acknowledgments to the following publications in which these poems first appeared, sometimes in slightly different forms: *IRIS*: "Withdrawal" (published as "Granted"); *The Iowa Journal of Cultural Studies:* "Two Figures Lying on a Bed with Attendants"; *The Colorado Review:* ". . . What a Lovely Way You Have of Putting Things," "Naked and Unashamed Are Two Different Moments"; *Denver Quarterly:* "Wafian as in Waven as in Wif"; *Delmar* 7: "Twelfth Night from the Willow Cabin," "Response to Sunlight"; *Delmar* 8: "Again, the Body as Temple," "On Gravity" (published as "Newton Falling"); *Seneca Review:* "Approaching Elegy"; *Xantippe*: "Mutatis Mutandis," "First Mardi Gras," "The Waiting"; *Electronic Poetry Review:* "Script Says Cry," "Self-Portrait with a Bee in My Mouth."

Thank you to The Rona Jaffe Foundation, whose generous award gave me time to work on this manuscript. Thank you to my teachers, especially Charles Wright, Rita Dove, Gregory Orr, Jorie Graham, James Galvin, Robert Hass, Brenda Hillman, Kathleen Pierce, Margo Figgins, and Bob McDonald. Sincere thanks to everyone who read and responded to these poems, especially Jerry Harp, Mark Szybist, Joanna Klink, Gabriela Rife, Kristin Morgan Pickering, Jen Scappetone, John Casteen, D.A. Powell, Molly Lou Freeman, Geoffrey G. O'Brien, Jan Weismiller, the Thursday night group, Kerri Dole, Margaret Cox, and Sarah Manguso. Thank you Connie Brothers and Deb West. To my friends and family, to Kathy, Bob, and Jim, my deepest gratitude for your generosity, support, and friendship.

For my parents

CONTENTS

—

It is quite possible that both versions were true, that he rejoiced at his release, and at the same time wept for her who released him. As a general rule, people, even the wicked, are much more naive and simple-hearted than we suppose. And we ourselves are, too.

—Fyodor Dostoyevsky
The Brothers Karamazov

At times it [is] necessary to grant the name of love to something less than love.

—Gina Berriault
"The Infinite Passion of Expectation"

MUTATIS MUTANDIS

Pebbles, leaves, rain—
they disappear into the river.
Even the shadows of the black branches above
(their bark peeling like thick burnt paper) disappear.

But we don't disappear:
Not into the breeze: it brushes
against the pale sides of our arms
(rustle of dry leaf against wood, quick suckle
of an inhale, cool shearing of cracks)—

Granted, this is not a world that keeps us.

Granted, there are some sadnesses
in which I do not long for God.

WHAT IF I COULD LOOK AT YOU

Despite some minor point of Genesis
     (the creation of angels)
the cars go by. Without
          hurry. Edging near me
even in my new dress,
     even with you, my everyone I love, right here
to talk to. The wet slide
     gossips by, bundles itself,
says good-night to itself—What if I could look

at you and not wonder
—what will happen?
but open you wide, without asking—

     All day I've wondered what I did
             to let
the hope in. I settle down at the window, look
at a branch,
     a wheel lying loose
and think "These
     can be made use of—"

When you slammed the lid down on the twilight
when you re-
     opened it,
        when the gnat-like courtship rattled
out, did you feel the footlights
          end? The cars
go by? They go by, we have lots
     of talk. I hope
something nice will happen.

—There are, after all, a few large stars overhead,
just so, irretrievable, and the cars go by
                              the obedient cars go by, can you
                    feel
the justice of it?—the headlights sliding across
                              the wall,
the glamour you managed—the look
                              of your lip just then—

NAKED AND UNASHAMED ARE TWO DIFFERENT MOMENTS

If I were a classical nude, the distance between my breasts
would be the same as the distance from my breasts to my navel,
from my navel to the division of my legs.

I accuse myself of transgressing.
What is it to drag a body
through the lush anger of atonement!

———

Always in the arms of something, the god is always
swaddled like the infant. The cloth on his hips.
Sometimes I believe I am transgressing.

When I consider the body in the manger
I feel it in my face: I must look the same way a hunter looks
when he decides to take an animal he has never seen before.

SWAMP

A low bleat starts up, like a huge swallowing.
I lie down in the darkness and listen.

He names the purring
starting with alligator—then, bullfrog—

I take his mouth
(flutter), make my high, light sounds—
So filled with lust for the influential phrase.

By day, we canoe the dark water.
He points up at the moist branches and says
osprey, egret, swallow-tailed-kite—
and I watch them eagerly, and I call to them
bird! bird! bird!

What the World Is For

Before I started to love you,
I tried to love the world:

the plump, dumb oranges that crushed
in my mouth, the waves that rolled upshore

until they were eyelid thin and purple.
And the girls who lined up to buy pops

in their small bright suits, the ones who slouched
and let their sandy thighs and ankles

go unbrushed: tried to love them
without seeming to, to watch

with an indifference I could wear.
Afternoons, they leaned against each other

picking out shapes in the clouds.
They weren't girls to throw their hair

before them, to dry it in the sun.
Still, their hair dried in the sun.

You could tell it would be a long time
before they would be bent

down to the kind of love
from which they could not right themselves.

It was a long time before I saw
the slivered moon is no scythe; it is not blade

or pool: we cannot see ourselves there.
It is only from here that it changes,

looks small as a thumbnail,
something to offer you

like the blonding shoreline, like myself.
As if that is what the world is for.

RAIMENT

Nothing subtle in
it. The pink
oleander pushing
up, each cup a
flushed petal
mocking the skin
on my neck. Red belladonna.
Parade of violets like rows
of girls being led
in only their bonnets
to a mirror.

I want to be stripped and
scrubbed down the way
one would scrub
a dog. Then I want to
be the dog: faithful,
plain. Will I wear
thin with vast
summer? I imagine
the disappearance of
leaves, of my palms
when they press
against the parts of
my body that
blush. Faithful and
plain and red
belladonna.

IDEALIZED HEAD

It lasts like this no matter what I do.
I scour shorelines, smooth my wet hair from the wind.
I try to keep you off and further off
but even the gulls, hung low in the clouds,
are gathering in the damp scent of your shadow.

The shore is littered with the small white skeletons
of sandcrabs, and foam that will stick to the lips.
I squat to examine a fish, its head
and tail gone, its skin still delicate.
I know how you hate to stop and stare like this,
but it didn't mind me there, and you
least of all, as you turned to watch the light fall
with a gesture only a woman would make
clasping your hands in amazement.

I think of the angel admonishing the man
for adoring him, that he should rather adore
the lord the angel served.

The clouds stir. My cheeks color to warm me.
There's a shell at the tail of my spine
that works like any shell.
Press your ear close. There's sand between my teeth.
I'm glad I have done nothing with my hair.

TWELFTH NIGHT FROM THE WILLOW CABIN

Can you see through the window, the moth
(color of old handkerchief) flickering up
through the dark—as if it would tell us something?
It doesn't. I continue to stack
the forks neck upon neck until they lie
still, they lie right. The moth flutters
lower. The cross-eyed cat approaches
with its tiny, bee-like mouth.

How can I say what it is to see it
brush you? As it denies me
even the smallest affection, I call it
Lucy, after the rich woman of Sicily
who spooned out
each of her eyes,
placed them on a platter,
and sent it to her suitor as a way of refusing. . . .

What separates self from the flutter
of longing? They don't fit
the way these spoons fit into each other.
They are more like knives that won't stack.
We do not own ourselves. We do
we know not what, and fear it; yes,
I believe miracles might change me,
but I mean conversion *from*.

O sweet burn-all-over,
we do not distinguish thirst
from hunger, nor the cat
at our feet, temptation from

the moth at the window, O sweet
burn I have always wanted
this pleasure, this end
—yet I intend to be gentle.

FIRST CONFESSION

So I bound the devil in chains and beat him.
Oh, he was sore. He admitted his poor
tactics. "Lady, have pity—on me—"
he begged, but I wagged my dogs on.

Or rather one dog. My sorry mutt
whose damp black nose nudged deep
into the demon's thigh. I raised his leg
and flopped it toward the dog who raised

her lips to growl. The devil tried to play
dead. He stared ahead, his one eye in,
the other hanging by its one black thread.
I wound my fingers round that strand, held down

his soft black head and yanked. Why should I pity
him—limp, one-eyed, and neckless?
Even the dog lost interest, plodding
to the window where the sugary snow

fell into the sloping branches
of a poplar. Or rather lots of poplars—
they went past where I could see—
the deepening, unbroken white stretched far

past me. I sat back, decided I
would watch the window as a picture
nailed there, fast. The frame hung still. The snow
blew back and forth and then it stopped.

The picture became just what I thought a picture
should: single slice of branch against a cloud.
No creep, no heave, nothing but reach
cut clean and clear into hereafter.

HIS ANIMALS

All those years behind windows
(his kisses pinned to my feet)

I knelt, I let him
look through me

and watched his many animals

but never tracked them,
never followed their strange feet

though I would call to them
sometimes, with bread crusts

remembering the squirrel through my window
who would not jump on my bed to wake me

to say walk carefully, yes
he has favored you, albino.

LONG AFTER THE DONKEY
AND DESERT

It does not surprise me, how happy I've grown.
Everyone has angels, but who has had an angel's child?
Woman with raven hair, you said, woman with fruit.
I was eating a pear when you came, so it sat,
half-eaten, for hours, lopsided, dry.

I was so young, so entirely agreeable to the task.
I bent so easily.
I bent over that boy so long
he began to mistake me for sky.
Yes, I cared for him, but it is you
who has stayed with me, after all.
It was not often I could say, here,
this is my boy, and take him by the ears.
But you have kept me combed for years,
you hollow out my door frames
with a precisely rectangular fierceness.
I lost him so uncontrollably, you understand,
and without credit for keeping him clean
and well-laundered. He became so tangled
and unshaven when he left
without so much as a handkerchief,
a way of saying good-bye. When he died,
when his unsandaled feet collapsed
at last across the sand,
I could not even part his hair.

So. Maternity was not like anything I had longed for
and you seemed so useless at first.
You fetched the most ordinary blocks of gray—
a brick for the mountains, a brick for the sea.

But how fortunate, these blocks, how they've propped us,
how they've made it so difficult to bend.
How fortunate, each angle
like an angle of my face. My face fades, closes.
The book in my lap does not ruffle.
The blades of your shoulders, your whole torso repeats,
but at least I have taught you edges.
You can lose a shapeless thing, dear heart;
the thing is to hold shapes that unfold.

I am paper unfolding, a fan of pages,
the staircase of my body, rectangle, square.
It does not surprise me: I am neat if not precise.
I'm almost content; I could almost sleep.
In another minute, I'll give you my chair.
I know you must be exhausted, so long
the living glue for yourself,
but again, darling, why do you clutch and tilt?

When you came, your lips were pale
and hard to see. You leaned close, filled my lap
with lilies even paler—remember?
Woman with raven hair, you called,
woman with fruit. I was so young.
So entirely agreeable to the task.

WHEN I WAS A SPOON IN
MY MOTHER'S KITCHEN

But what a luxury to be without hands,
stiff and lazy as all utensils are
with only the back crook of a head
and a neck silver and long as an unraveled snail.
Not even an eye to watch her
rinse another fork
and place it neatly beside me.
We're clean as the chicken bones in their water.
When they simmer, she sits at the piano
and begins—

⸻

I can think so clearly,
it's like dreaming.
How she would call my name,
brush my hair, till we became each other's
possession. Her lashes, my cheeks, her brows,
my lips: how the melody winds itself down.
Her shoulders, my arms, my chest,
her waist—each key
a representative joy—
the range becomes sparser; she picks two C's
and trills them. Her thighs, my legs,
my ankles, her feet. A two-hand chord
blends, deems itself worthy to linger.
We would make a beautiful woman.

I can think so clearly:
another cadence thinks it is dying,
tries to find a pattern:

The treble winging itself above
the three note baseline:
Take me home, take me strong, take me there;
the treble wanders, nervous in how it precedes itself,
each key an unpried oyster
touched, touched again. . . .

I can think so clearly, I think
we are two sharp bass tones that do not recur
as the bass drops to a single note
obsessive as breath. She is calling me moon-face again.
Then the bass creeps, as slow pattern replaces,
pounds itself into, so easily replaces, pounds
down an octave, creeps. . . .
As the treble searches itself out in scales.
Now softer. Now almost not there.

CRYLIGHT

We like loss to be quiet.
Outside, flowers with lemon-stained throats
smack noiselessly at the breeze though their mouths
don't close, no they cower
to closing.

When I speak, my voice speaks
over me, its light notes
ligatures to make you
calm again. To relieve
each sound of its wail
you knock, I exhale—
we like loss to be quiet.
This entails no loveliness. If I loved you less,
I would be aggressively lovely.

Outside, each flower makes a face.
My face makes faces but each
looks, you say, the same.
What stupor kissed me,
revoked me, left me bent?
Is there assent in me?
We like loss to be quiet.

VIA NEGATIVA

Sometimes it's too hard with words or dark or silence.
Tonight I want a prayer of high-rouged cheekbones
and light: a litany of back-lit figures,
lithe and slim, draped in fabrics soft and wrinkleless and pale
as onion slivers. Figures that won't stumble or cough:
sleek kid-gloved Astaires who'll lift
ladies with glamorous sweeps in their hair—
They'll bubble and glitter like champagne.
They'll whisper and lean and waltz and wink effortlessly
as figurines twirling in music boxes, as skaters in their dreams.

And the prayer will not be crowded.
You'll hear each click of staccato heel
echo through the glassy ballrooms—too few shimmering skirts;
the prayer will seem to ache
for more. But the prayer will not ache.
When we enter, its chandeliers and skies
will blush with pleasure. Inside
we will be weightless, and our goodness will not matter
in a prayer so light, so empty it will float.

Monologue to be Spoken
by an Archangel

Snow! & snow of Our Lady!
Know the lamb

has dropped into sleep, numb,
stiff as a courtier, the lamb

{Hands indicating the motions of waves}

is not with you.

{A long time passes}

. . .and Our Lady grows
distressingly simple, caught
beneath stones, her white
bruises. . . . Who has

{Indicating the eyes}

not been God's thief?

{Disappears}

Our Lady! is dizzy,
ill, among sparrows—She
is stripped and salts herself.
When she cries, she cries
out to . . .

{Indicating absence}

                    . . . Who
has not been God's wife?

AGAIN, THE BODY AS TEMPLE

A television lovely is forsaken by a man
and gestures wildly at her heart.
I wish I had inherited such drama.

Beyond the impossible nose on each Madonna,
there is a body curious with grasping.
The Madonna stays still

the stunned, the silent darling.
Shame, shame, this lilt in her arms, she ought
not to tilt her chin, but rear
up toward him

or shiver at least.

When everything is proper with imminent purpose
resistance has no part in it.
Saints have no excuses for flinching, for feeling
so forsaken as to
cry out—

Lie back and the body will happen.
If you need to make it proper you must speak.

In darkness
        the world is what my body touches.

It is only the body and only the body
as the sparrows stir below my belly. . . .
Such dull birds.

———

. . . they do not cry out.
They are the usual shrills.

———

But love requires performance:
When the soldiers raised up Jesus
to leave him perched, exposed,
he could have finished with the calm
what they do, I do. Love could have remained
the arranged thing, the pronouncement.
Why the sudden anguish (where I rush to him),
the swelling in music?

It would have been easier to give in
to the shape assigned him, not to have summoned
the cry—

to have given into the quiet. . .
(while seduction was still a form of disappointment).

Script Says Cry

They look more alert and patient now.
They quiet around me and wait.
I must be frail here, summon the appearance
as it is a cold day, as the curtains are thick with dust—

But I am all interruption.
I arch my back a trifle, my mouth embarrassed and open—

A metal teaspoon slants in a glass cup;
I lean on a chair at the same angle.
I try to hold still. My leaning begins to swoon—
I touch my head with one fingertip, flinch.
I bring my mouth to my shoulder and nudge it.

A handkerchief falls. The moment is still going on—
the lamp at the end of the table is still coating the room
with its expected flush, and the natural heat of my body,
though conscious of great sweetness,

is growing colder as the moment presses closer, against me,
with eyes intent on me. . .
but they are tired of me now.

I look at them more directly than I have for several minutes.
To continue past the moment I say *I am thirsty*
and continue past the moment.

AGAINST BITTERNESS

To begin I peel their socks
          like the thin skins
of oranges, using my thumbnails
          to get under to

a cool swelled
          flesh that has
no scent. Through the window comes
          lilac, it leans

into us as the light
          blinks like small epileptic
stars through the trees
          by whose low branches

the lower roof, is, necessarily
          slapped. The wind passes,
the rings on my fingers
          tighten, and the ladies

in these stiff bodies
          are obligated, now, to let me
bathe them. One
          at a time I strip them

but not of their sense
          of sin—their heads bow,
the windows glint
          at the imbecile

sun, did I say
          sin? I meant how they live
by hands which snap them
          out of their garments into

the straps of chairs that wheel
            into a bath where I
lift each arm
            and leg to a stretch

I hold open and
            lather. And rinse. And
longer, I don't let
            go. I keep

rinsing, I have each lady
            lean her head
back, slowly as she
            can, stiff

lilac, to what intent
            did its scent
enter the window
            which held the blue beginning

of a shoulder? almost seizing
            the lady, her hair
drying now, brushing
            her bare scrubbed neck—

Stiff lilac, is it really so
            clean to breathe
out, in the heat—to be
            so chronically scent?

IN THE GLARE OF THE GARDEN

Yes, the open mouth
of your watering can, it
reminds me of you, of
rushing toward
smallness, toward
a bright and yellowish
color. Its mouth is smaller
than any part of it,
smaller than any of those red
or yellow petals. It
reminds me of me, of
smallness that seems
closable, but isn't. Go ahead
and tilt it, keep it
up over the zinnias—it
isn't empty. The zinnias
have their tongues out now almost
completely, let's have it
go to them. I don't think it has
ever seen them before,
let's have it
hold in the air a little
longer—it doesn't know
the smell yet, yes,
I think you want emptiness
also, let's have it. And the zinnias
open and spark and unregarding it goes
out to them.

RESPONSE TO SUNLIGHT

for Jerry Harp

The more mature this light becomes
the more it holds: the whole sunk
seat of your chair, save where
the shadow of its thin wood arm

reaches across and past it to
the center of the coffee table.
In between, the air doesn't hold shadow.
But the shadow gets through to

continue its line, unbleached. Beneath,
I think I can see that piece of beam fallen
into the elaborate design of the carpet.
But it's unclear. I return to tracing

the line. It's not unlike the way
I trace myself back to myself
after returning from spaces that have
no place in me. Not unlike the way

I trace over moments with you when you
are no one I recognize. The line
disappears and reappears
to become exactly what it was

though reaching only so far—
for which, it seems, the light is responsible.
I'd like to be able to say this to you:
we know the light is responsible.

FIRST MARDI GRAS

Even as he levels the gun at me,
places it firmly against my temple
and cocks it, I don't believe I'll die.

Quiet, I want to say, quiet:
I'm trying to think. But he's not talking.

The metal is cool against my skin, the pressure
makes me think the gun is heavy—

—

With that jagged branch above us,
the air heavy, damp, just after a rain,
and a crowd gathering, drunk, a crowd
near enough, an electric cable crossing the sky
like a vein, someone hurling an obscenity,
someone just about to turn around—

—

From a distance: as if I am an instrument he is tuning,
or as if (adjusting his mask) he is adjusting an instrument
to look through me—

—

The sky is measled with stars.
There was a soul, a god, too, that I meant
to concoct.

I look down.
The shattered glass doesn't know
to glitter in the moonlight.
It doesn't seem right it wouldn't know.

The first float appears: the crowds erupt
like static: Bacchus, fruit-crowned, freckled,
raising his goblet; Bacchus plush in his white gown,
with a flick of mortal fans behind him—

I look down.
I give up my purse,
gather my hair, help him
remove, from my neck, everything—
Tomorrow, Lent.

Who told me, who told me,
God was personal? Plausibility,
tick-tock—and the parades begin.

THE WAY ONE PICKS UP A SHELL
ON THE BEACH

I come home to a room filled
with smoke and thick piles
of mannequins: some pieces
naked, some swaddled. They
are almost recognizable: leg
of Mary, head of Joseph, two
left arms of the boy Jesus.
Their burning is slow. I must
put them out. I begin
to carry them by their necks
or ankles. I am careful not to
drag them. They flare, turn to quick
dust in the yard. I keep on
until my friend comes to tell me
it is dark. She wears a sheer
blue veil. I can see all of her
ribs. She takes me to bed.
When I am almost asleep
a man the size of a child appears.
His skin resembles the inside
of a conch shell. He says something
about the fire. He lifts my friend's
hair and examines her from several
angles. He begins to undress her.
She uses only her hands
to cover herself. I put my hands
over her eyes. "It isn't a woman," I say.
"It is a waterfall." "Oh?" he says,
settling down on the bed, pulling out
a pair of spectacles. He puts them
on. He says, "Drink."

THE MOUTHS OF CARP

Seem to gasp that they are unfinished.

Below the bridge, above the gray surface of the water,
their heads upright as candles.
                    They open and reopen at their mouths.

I meant not to hesitate:
meant to feed them, but the way their mouths gape,
almost whine—

Look: the carp can withstand fasting.
Like the glass eyes of saints, their eyes
have cooled into unfocus,
their bodies have become sleek, their movements quick
and agile, and I'm glad just to watch their mouths
glisten, dumb as halos.

Approaching Elegy

It's hard to believe you are dying: like looking
at a Jamesian scene, skipping past happiness
to a garden bench beyond the trees. You fill the form
of *heroine*: you sit in your black dress, too tired to imagine
      the rest of yourself.
                An old suitor appears, grabs you possibly

too forcefully by the wrists (he is still impossibly
in love—). You disengage your wrists. He leans forward, looks
into your eyes, which you close—as if you were all by yourself.
He moves closer, talking very fast about happiness.
      He places his cloak on your shoulders, imagines
          he'll rescue you. Around you, forms

grow darker: house, branch, hydrangea. Above you, freckled
    expanses of leaves form
the beginnings of barbed, lopsided shrouds—a possible
solace. If only his kiss could please you, I wouldn't need to imagine
past the clean architecture of the story. And perhaps it is wrong to look
      past that. Wrong to ask about happiness.
          Past midnight, he continues to offer himself.

Before, he had offered aimless passion, but now (you see it for yourself)
he has an idea: he points into the darkness. He is grave, formal.
The dark has swallowed the long shadows of the oaks (though not
    your unhappiness)
—and it is about to swallow you. Soon, it will no longer be possible
      (there is just one more page to turn) for me to look
          through your eyes, so I would like to imagine

for you: something past tragedy. Just as I would like to imagine
that we are not in danger, that we have selves
more solid than stars, that we are safe in the pages of books we can
    reopen to look
at each other. Except that we are not women formed
        of words, but of impossible
            longings. What was it that you wanted besides happiness?

You are dying. I have no ideas about happiness
and no patience to imagine
it possible.
Soon you will not be the heroine; you will not be yourself.
        And it's not that you've lost the formula; your form
            is losing you. Look

at how brave you are: I imagined the great point was to be happy,
    as happy as possible
with the quick forms that imagine us—but the last time I looked
there you were—distant and bright in the not so blue darkness,
    imagining yourself.

HEAVEN IN MINIATURE

for Tina Wang (1984-2001)

After the crash, I tried imagining:

After they lift you out of the car—(I begin)
you wake beneath a cypress-flooded sky,
etcetera. Or, in a field, sunlit
immense, where a white-haired, white-robed shepherd
calls out to you, unbuckles your sandaled feet.
Etcetera, etcetera, I try.

———

After the oarsmen lift Odysseus
out of the hollow hull, after they set
him down asleep on the sand and leave him there,
he wakes beneath an olive tree spreading
its leaves in a mist. It's not what he was promised.
The land looks strange, unearthly strange
and unforgivable. He's sick for home
and doesn't recognize the way the thick
low mist sticks to the sea-raged, ragged shore.
Hardly recognizes the treasure that sits
around him like spilled confetti. He begins,
therefore, to count. It's all he can think to do:
to count up what is there; to stack gold coin
on coin. Everything he remembers is there,
but then, he can't remember. So he counts;
he counts and does not see the shepherd boy
approaching (disguised Athena—his Athena),
ready to give him a new body; doesn't
see he's about to recognize the skyline,
about to find all who are dear to him

unharmed. He's weeping, kneeling on the shore
of his own country, trying to figure
what's lost. Along the sand he lays out each
bright piece of woven clothing, polished bronze,
each surpassingly beautiful ornament
and counts and counts and finds that he lacks nothing.

WITHDRAWAL

Mountains, rocks fall upon us and hide us from the wrath of the Lamb.
At the present moment I deserve this wrath. —SIMONE WEIL

Even pebbles want to break.
See them kneel, see them bend without necks
their round scalps to the sun.
Hear them beg: Light, send lightning.

The fish know, in their heavy water.
They swallow hooks.

It is the itch to scratch myself rawer than meat,
the shaking after sedation.
The itch that transforms a body to clubs of flesh.
And I could keep the drowning that neat,
that packaged,
if I could wear blood like apples do.

I try to sit and pray.
I praise whatever name I can:
God, mercy.
Make me hands of little fingers, make me pine.

God, throw me a line.
The drowning takes too long.

I dream my body is bald as a Buddha, bald as a child, the
    bare-fingered children
fingered by all the cool, cold hands that go fingering.

Yes, I am tired of the bleating, and no,
I cannot swallow even this bit of brown bread.

So mutts, pack rats, dirty dogs,
here is my throat.

If there are bones you cannot swallow,
leave teeth marks.
If everywhere I went, Lamb,
you would only grant me wrath, rocks,
a cliff, a flight, a leap . . . .

I would leave you then
if only the rush of the wind streaming between my teeth
could thrill me.
I would leave you if anything could.

APOLOGY

I didn't mean to say so much to you.
I should have thought to let the evening end
by looking at the stars subdued

into their antique blue and alabaster hues.
Such looking would have fit with my intent.
I didn't mean to speak that way to you.

If I could take it back, I'd take it, undo
it, and replace it with the things I meant
to give—not what I let slip (it's true)

like any pristine star of ornamental hue.
I do not always do what I intend.
I didn't mean to say so much to you.

It slipped before I saw, before I knew.
Or do we always do what we intend?
Perhaps it's true and all along I knew

what I was saying—but how I wanted you.
I should have thought to let the evening end.
The placid stars seemed filled and then subdued
by what I did and did not want to do.

ON GRAVITY

I bought a very beautiful hand-colored book on diseases of the mouth
To capture the sensation of mouth as sunset.
People say you forget about death, but you don't.
My lips curve upward in spite of themselves.
Can you smell the cadaver in me?
The hey sugar, my cherry
The waves under my tongue, the starfish pushing its stomach
Through its mouth, the waves under my tongue
The hey sugar, my cherry
Can you smell the cadaver in me?
My lips curve upward in spite of themselves.
People say you forget about death, but you don't.
To capture the sensation of mouth as sunset
I bought a very beautiful hand-colored book on diseases of the mouth.

TRAIN STATION, RENO:
EARLY DECEMBER

Never mind the train was late
  or the desert behind: the dusk
was good. Your truck pulling
  away from me was one shade
less visible, unremarkable
  as the hairpin I kept trying
not to touch—pin
  and then sigh pressing
like the two sides of that desert:
  sky and not sky. Sky
and not. The windows glittered
  with the city's faint fluorescent
shapes: triangles, diamonds,
  clowns, the fantastical ladies of luck.
They flashed triumphantly; and the darker
  it became the more the shapes
would not alter; they brightened
  but the lights did not flurry,
did not break the clear glass
  into clerestory, oh. I
was going back. There was
  a line to buy tickets (though it was hardly
line at all) and a woman beside me
  crocheting ornaments.
And she was young, I mean,
  she was almost *bride,* almost
that solid, unavoidable
  shape. The tracks
were *line:* clear and straight
  and endless. Whoever
you were when you showed me

that full half-world of stars
in which I remembered nothing but *sky*—
  gone. The woman began
to sew sequins onto crochet:
  a crocheted angel, white,
white, like Cleopatra dropping
  the pearls into her glass.
Then raising the vinegar up.

"... What a Lovely Way You Have of Putting Things"

The unthinkable has happened.

Meanwhile, you are reading the paper.
Meanwhile, hundreds of women in bed sheets

are descending like wrapped treats from a piñata.
They cry out their names and point to themselves over and over.
Catherine, Anne, Angela Merici. Some of them blow

into silver trumpets, spit through the holes in their hands.
Cecilia plays a harp and sings "The angels are bitches,
the gods are sluts—" Brave Joan cries, "Let us beset the just one

for he is obnoxious to us." They snarl,
fling their bare arms. Therese tangles her hair up, chides
"barstool of my affection—" little Maria Goretti moans "with all
my heart,

with all my strength" as pretty Dymphna snaps
a leather belt above your left ear
whispering, "Pray for us who have recourse to thee."

I won't explain these angry virgins.
I am against you, at ease, cheerful.
I am sincere. Literature is falling away.
I am entirely sincere.

OUR LADY OF THE MILK

You're the head injury I've always longed for,
what I call thinking.

You ease my chin up. I try to recall
star, water,

water with wash,
your sleeves to your elbows, you

are what I call thinking now,
your face thick, irreproachable as you walk

the long keyhole each evening
to feed me, with cups

since my hands are no good with spoons . . . .
Do you have no desire

to leave me? Is it that my hands are no good
with spoons? Haven't I always looked

for the cup? With the cup down, I make myself
into shapes, into hull, into rack. In this way

the changes I want I don't have
to suffer. I am—
as you know—apostle, and the very best kind—

plain. Plain. Don't you want to leave me
undisgraced? My eyes your albescence—

You are what I call thinking.
The injury I long for.

THE TECHNIQUE
OF THE LIFELIKE

I had imagined death thrillingly:
my arms held behind to restrain their frivolous occasions,
the whole of me bending
like a tall yellow lily before you.

Yet see how my hands go on with their thoughts.
See how I fold and fold my handkerchief.

I am not a great lady.
I don't swoon with love.

My stricken, I cannot render you as you
move quickly toward your skillful execution,
your shoulders tossing their indifference to the dark,
your face overlaid with stage effects.
You grow irresistibly small. Your hands and feet expire.
This is where sculpture also fails, this is where I turn
wholly unattached and without debt.

What is the use of crowning you in glory?

Now my fingers make bowls for rain: in your honor: hope for noth-
ing.
We knew our disposition long ago.

THE WAITING

On the Roman girl's sarcophagus, cupids
hold a wreath around her image.
The cupids don't look at her, but down
and to the side—as if modest;
but the way their mouths are parted
keeps them from seeming so.

And though they hold this wreath around her,
they don't stand steadily, but float, kicking their legs high
to display their intimate parts
as their bellies lop generously downward.

At the corners of the box, Eros takes Psyche's cheeks
in both his hands. Her hand is firmly on the curve
of his belly—

Who has waited longest for this kiss?
The girl's image—though the face is entirely corroded—
is the bust of one who could sit up straight and pose.

Her crypt is infant-sized
but the bereft did not imagine her so small.
They inscribed her fully formed

as if to tempt the virile angels past the wreath. . . .

—

What if the inanimate were forced into motion?

If Eros finally lowered his face,
finally felt the lips pulse beneath him, the nimble
fingers stroke his belly—

If the cupids, roused, dropped the wreath
and turned to face the girl—

What if they didn't know how to feel,
not even how they were supposed to feel.

Imagine: there would be no mercy in them.

WĀFIAN AS IN WAVEN
AS IN WĪF

When I met the soldier, I asked what the shooting meant.
She said, the target afterward.
Being accurate. Perfectly accurate.

———

The soldier wetted the wave in my hair.
She said, "I want to do *that.*"

———

I put on a sheer wave dress for her.
Wave as in "girl."

———

We could see the wave coming toward us—
The purplish surface fluttering
free at one end—

———

My tongue was a wave.
Swept as it dove.
Said "infant. . .".

———

The wavering went on.
Waves endways, sideways, frontways—

———

The candles were embarrassed.

They made stars to cover themselves.

———

So when the soldier began with me
I waved as in "wave down."
"No fish, no fish in the bed," I ordered.

———

I looked for water. I wanted to spread her fins wide
and throw her into waves of water
even though I saw how sad this made her.

———

She said, "Is wave abandon?"

———

I rocked her to sleep.
A wave half locked in my throat—
(wave as in "wave up").
It is true she was drooling.

———

I rocked her to sleep.
I was calm and my body was helplessly so.
Lime and ice in our glasses.
When I suffer for her, I will write it differently.

SELF-PORTRAIT WITH A BEE
IN MY MOUTH

I said *no*—and then it was abuzz inside me,
all wings, restless—

Raw lust for romance—

You were undressing, peeling off
the thick socks you'd sweat through.

It wasn't you I'd refused.
You smelled of cut grass, your back ached,
you closed your eyes for a moment

before I kissed you in what I believed was silence.
But the buzz started up, hovered
as I searched out your lips, as I pulled you toward me,
as I *succumbed*

to the force of your lips . . . .

Though I kissed, of course, you,
not *the forceful domination of his lips.*

Like a bee in a glass jar, my mind buzzes—
But the bee is in my mouth.

The buzzing, sometimes, is so quiet
I don't know it's there.

I've tried to tempt it out.
Weeding the garden, I nuzzle my cheek
against the thick-veined petals, fragrances
rising like incense.
Only more fly in.

I have only to touch you to be *suddenly lifted*
into the cradle of your arms, to *surrender completely*. . . .

I lose you in the buzzing.

(All wings, restless,
and a kind of anger in it:
an open flower, a prairie rose
a little past bloom and still unattended—)

See how close a body can come to having wings.

They pick and play me, as if I were made for them.

What was I made for, then?

Two Figures Lying on a Bed with Attendants

Left Panel

The first sits. He crosses his legs and stares.
He has been attending them a long time.
He has learned, at last, to position himself.
His arms must stay close to his body.
See, he demonstrates, *I do this even in a chair, dropping*
the short flat bone in my elbow.
You have no proper . . .
                              while he goes on like this
leaning forward, drawing himself back

a bird is springing from the hole in the floor,
is darting toward the couple—It is a stork.
It craves nakedness. It is ready to complete the man's movement.

RIGHT PANEL

There are more in attendance.
A man dressed in a gray suit, a black shoe,
his left arm bent as if to conduct a closing
of the bed, the two spines heaped across it—
he is not a man to spend nights showing nothing
but the frivolous small of his back.

He has managed a tactful arrangement of his spilling, it sits
at his heels like a dog, its face that of a dog,
it is complicit with the man,
they leer in the direction of the bed—

If he had a mouth to voice his open face,
he would say *sluts* and *children*—
you are not enough to know what is coming.

CENTRAL PANEL

The one good eye of the room
wide open on the pillow, on the most legible head.

Why else would two people shut
their green blinds and half
fall into each other?

No, it is true this time.
They are loved.

In Tennessee I Found a Firefly

Flashing in the grass; the mouth of a spider clung
    to the dark of it: the legs of the spider
held the tucked wings close,
    held the abdomen still in the midst of calling
with thrusts of phosphorescent light—

When I am tired of being human, I try to remember
    the two stuck together like burrs. I try to place them
central in my mind where everything else must
    surround them, must see the burr and the barb of them.
There is courtship, and there is hunger. I suppose
    there are grips from which even angels cannot fly.
Even imagined ones. *Luciferin, luciferase.*
    When I am tired of only touching,
I have my mouth to try to tell you
    what, in your arms, is not erased.

NOTES

The Latin phrase "Mutatis Mutandis" literally means "that having been changed which had to be changed." This phrase is commonly translated "with the necessary changes."

"Long After the Donkey and Desert" was inspired by *Dos Mujeres,* a cubist painting by Diego Rivera, in which I saw a kind of annunciation scene, or rather the aftermath of annunciation. The poem is informed by three notions of Gabriel: 1. Gabriel is said to possess 140 pairs of wings. 2. Gabriel also means "divine husband" 3. Gabriel is believed by many to be the only female archangel. In the poem, Mary speaks.

"Approaching Elegy": The heroine to whom the "you" of the poem is compared is Isabel Archer in Henry James' *Portrait of a Lady.* This poem is for Veronica Ateaga.

"Train Station, Reno: Early December": According to one legend, Cleopatra wagered that she could consume, at a single meal, the value of a million sisterces. She supposedly won the bet by dropping a million sisterces worth of pearls into a glass of vinegar and drinking dissolved pearls.

The title, ". . . What a Lovely Way You Have of Putting Things," is taken from Anaïs Nin.

"Wāfian as in Waven as in Wīf": The words wave [ME waven<OE wāfian] and wife [ME<OE wīf] both derive from the same Old Norse word *veifa,* to vibrate.

The italicized phrases in "Self Portrait with a Bee in my Mouth" were taken from *The Romance Writers' Phrase Book* by Jean Kent and Candance Shelton.

"Two Figures Lying on a Bed with Attendants" is based on a painting of the same title by Francis Bacon, oil and pastel on canvas, 1968.

"In Tennessee I Found a Firefly": Luciferin is the chemical substance present in the cells of fireflies that produces light when oxidized under the catalytic effects of luciferase.

RECENT TITLES FROM ALICE JAMES BOOKS

Alice James Books has been publishing exclusively poetry since 1973. One of the few presses in the country that is run collectively, the cooperative selects manuscripts for publication through both regional and national annual competitions. New regional authors become active members of the cooperative, participating in the editorial decisions of the press. The press, which historically placed an emphasis on publishing women poets, was named for Alice James, sister of William and Henry, whose fine journal and gift for writing went unrecognized within her lifetime.

Typeset and Designed by Dede Cummings
Printed by Thomson-Shore